Following in their steps

Short biographies for the Holy Days of
the Revised Common Lectionary

Eleanor and Rachel Sayers

First published in 1997 by
KEVIN MAYHEW LTD
Rattlesden
Bury St Edmunds
Suffolk IP30 0SZ

© 1997 Eleanor and Rachel Sayers

The right of Eleanor and Rachel Sayers to be identified as the authors
of this work has been asserted by them in accordance
with the Copyright, Designs and Patents Act 1988.

All rights reserved. No part of this publication may be reproduced,
stored in a retrieval system, or transmitted, in any form or by any means,
electronic, mechanical, photocopying, recording or otherwise,
without the prior written permission of the publisher.

ISBN 1 84003 073 9
Catalogue No 1500145

0 1 2 3 4 5 6 7 8 9

Front cover: *The Life of St Augustine* (fresco) (detail)
by Benozzo di Lese di Sandro Gozzoli (1420-97). San Agostino,
San Giminiano/Bridgeman Art Library, London

Cover design by Jaquetta Sergeant
Typesetting by Louise Hill
Printed in Great Britain

FOREWORD

All the people in this book are remembered on Holy Days in the Church calendar because of the way they gave their lives and energies to be used by God. Some are ancient and some modern, some are well known and others quite obscure; some were loved by all who met them, others were feared and hated. God had given them all different gifts, and when these people allowed God to be in control of their lives, amazing things happened. As we recall these very different lives throughout the year, we can reflect on how we are letting our Maker use the gifts he has given us for his purposes.

The life sketches we have written try to put this across. They are intentionally short, to enable them to be read aloud, printed on handouts or in a church magazine, and they are written so that the language is suitable for all ages. As the Church of today, we can be encouraged and inspired by these ordinary people made extraordinary through God's grace.

ELEANOR AND RACHEL SAYERS

JANUARY

2nd   **Basil the Great**

Basil the Great lived c. 330-79. He grew up in a rather holy family with six of his close relatives becoming saints. He became a bishop and responsibly sorted out his flock. He is famous for his theological writings which cleverly integrated the secular outlooks of the day into a new theological outlook, and for the way in which he was not afraid to roll up his sleeves and live out his words in action.

2nd   **Gregory of Nazianzus**

Gregory of Nazianzus was born the son of a bishop in 329 and died a bishop himself in 389. After reluctantly being ordained priest, he ran off to his friend Basil the Great to hide from his duties for ten weeks. From his own experience he developed understanding of the duties of the priest, which he wrote down to help others. Later in life he transformed his house in Constantinople into a church and restored orthodoxy to the city. After retiring he wrote religious poems in his garden.

2nd   **Seraphim of Sarov**

Seraphim was a Russian monk who lived 1759-1833. Much of his life was spent in a solitary existence in a hermitage after seeing visions of the Virgin Mary and the apostles. Here he practised subsistence agriculture to support himself, and advised those who came to him with both understanding and firmness. His life put a great emphasis on the importance of the Holy Spirit in people's lives, and the importance of a life of service and poverty.

2nd   **Vedanayagam Samuel Azariah**

Living from 1874 until just before Indian independence, in 1945, Vedanayagam Samuel was the first Indian bishop of the Anglican church in India, Burma and Ceylon (now

JANUARY

Sri Lanka). He was a firm believer in co-operation between the foreign workers in the Church and those who were Indian, and also a great advocate of the development of indigenous leadership in the Church which must have been a great help after independence.

10th **William Laud**

Archbishop from 1633 until he was beheaded in 1640, William struggled with a country on the brink of civil war. He believed in the autocracy of the king and the opinions he held turned many against him. When he introduced the Prayer Book in Scotland so that there would be a common order of service everywhere, a revolt started which led to the English Civil War. However, it is clear that he valued what he felt was right so highly that the consequences became immaterial.

11th **Mary Slessor**

Mary was born in 1848 and worked as a mill girl in Dundee throughout her childhood and early adulthood. However, her great dream in life was to become a missionary, and she was accepted to teach in Calabar, Nigeria, by the United Presbyterian Church in 1876. She spent many years there teaching and was very popular with the Nigerians. She was known as 'Great Mother', and her love for people brought many of them closer to God.

12th **Aelred of Hexham**

In 1134 Aelred became a monk at the abbey of Rievaulx and, despite bad health, enthusiastically followed the austere regime there. He was so respected and well liked by his fellow monks there that he eventually became abbot. With his gift of human friendship, he put a human face to Cistercian monasticism. As a result, his house grew to be the largest in England, and he was able to befriend and help many others by his preaching and his letters.

JANUARY

12th   **Benedict Biscop**

Benedict was born to a noble Northumbrian family in 628, and after visits to the Holy Land and to Rome he decided to become a monk. He created his own community based on the Benedictine rules, but with a special emphasis on beauty. Feeling that lovely surroundings would help those worshipping, he brought in Frankish stonemasons, glassmakers and craftsmen (who in turn passed their expertise on to those living nearby), and he bought books from Rome, and also paintings to help devotions.

13th   **Hilary**

Hilary was born into a rich family who were not Christian, but after a lot of studying he came to the conclusion that there was a God, and that Jesus was both man and God. This approach led him to develop logical and learned arguments to prove the Christian faith. He became a bishop and steadfastly defended the orthodoxy of the Church both with his skills as a speaker and with his writings. He died in 367.

13th   **Kentigern (Mungo)**

It is clear from the legends surrounding Kentigern's life that he must have been a very influential and much-loved figure before his death in 612. That he was a monk and bishop known by a pet name, Mungo, amongst all those he served points to a very easily approachable man who inspired affection and led by love, not only in Strathclyde where he was a bishop, but also in Cumbria where he was exiled.

13th   **George Fox**

After his own very personal experience of God, George held this more important than conventions set up by the established Church. His magnetic personality brought many to his way of thinking and the Society of Friends was founded. There was a concentration on social issues as

JANUARY

well as theology, but, regarded as a threat, many members underwent imprisonment – George himself was imprisoned eight times between 1649 and 1673. However, the members were not discouraged by this and kept on worshipping God.

17th **Antony of Egypt**

Living from 251 to 356, Antony sold all his possessions at the age of twenty to go and live with the ascetics in the desert. From 286 to 306 he led a completely solitary life, living on bread and water, and fasting. Out of this he showed that the love of God must be put first before all other things, and the strength of his argument, based on real experience, impressed even the philosophers.

17th **Charles Gore**

Charles, ordained priest in 1878, came from an Anglo-Catholic background with a belief in the Anglican Church's apostolic succession, and with a strong interest in social reform. He also had an abiding interest in science, and this led him to try to marry theology with all that was known of science and history. His courage to question assumptions and to work with what seemed to be threatening facts led to more secure knowledge.

19th **Wulfstan**

Wulfstan's life, spanning from c. 1008 to 1095, covered a period of great political upheaval. In his education he excelled both in piety and sport, and this hands-on godliness was apparent throughout his life. He refused a rich church in favour of building up a small priory, and later became much involved with the politics of the day, supporting William the Conqueror, and campaigning for the abolition of the slave trade from Bristol to Viking Ireland.

JANUARY

20th **Richard Rolle**

Born in Yorkshire in *c.* 1300, Richard began a degree at Oxford university but, annoyed by the lack of depth and reality in the subjects, left before completion. He became a hermit, and from this time spent alone he was able to experience a great closeness with God. This led him to write books in everyday English with the purpose of leading women into the amazing union with God that he had experienced.

21st **Agnes**

Agnes was martyred at the age of thirteen in *c.* 304. She had promised God that she would stay a virgin, and when marriage was suggested found death an acceptable alternative. Even though she was young, she had a deep love for God and obviously also a deep realisation that the love relationship she enjoyed with God would beat any other. Her death bore witness to the depth of God's love that she experienced.

22nd **Vincent of Saragossa**

During the persecutions from Diocletian and Maximian, a deacon called Vincent was under intense pressure. He knew that if he refused to deny his faith he could lose his life, but also recognised that doing what God wanted was more important than his physical well-being. He was imprisoned and partially starved but when given the let-out clause of performing a sacrifice, refused. In 304 he was tortured on the rack, burnt on a grid-iron, imprisoned, set in stocks, and died, to the last refusing to deny his God.

24th **Francis de Sales**

Born in 1567, Francis de Sales' good education could have led to a distinguished career in many professions but Francis' deep wish was to become a priest. He was ordained and

JANUARY

soon became well known for his kind dealings with the poor and for his skills as a preacher. Many were converted by his attractive life of love and understanding. He gently nudged people to deeper self-sacrifice and to a deeper understanding of God's love, both through his writings and through personal contact.

26th **Timothy**

Timothy grew up in a Christian household with both his mother and his grandmother teaching him how to love his God. From this early beginning, living in Christian fellowship as a child, he was able to offer fellowship and support to Paul as he grew older. Paul recognised the young man's potential, and his training manual came in the form of Paul's letters to Timothy. He became the first Bishop of Ephesus and was martyred because of his protests against pagan festivals.

26th **Titus**

Titus, a friend and companion of Paul, lived in the first century. After being with Paul for many years he became his secretary and was able to support him in his work. Paul obviously had a high regard for his abilities, as he was sent on a number of difficult missions, including being sent to organise the Church in Crete. It seems as if he succeeded, as it is believed that he became the first bishop there.

28th **Thomas Aquinas**

This well-known and much-loved saint was born in c. 1225. When he attempted to become a Dominican monk, he was held captive by his family for a year, but eventually managed to join the order. He was a great thinker and prayer, activities he carried out with much enthusiasm and concentration. He wrote many books, in cramped handwriting on little parchment due to the poverty of the monks, and these have served to inspire and enrich the Church.

JANUARY

30th   Charles

Charles, King of England from 1625-1649, believed in his right as king to rule, and did not agree with the concept of parliament. He also felt that religious life in England was changing and he did not want to see that happen. However, these views obviously led him into major problems with parliament, which brought about the Civil War. Throughout all of the problems, and even to his execution, Charles refused to be swayed from what he felt was right.

31st   John Bosco

John was born in Italy in 1815. He became a Roman Catholic priest and was very concerned about the education of the poor. In 1859, along with twenty-two other like-minded friends, he founded the Salesian Teaching Order to educate those who were too poor to find the funds to gain an education. The Order grew as more and more people realised the need and it spread across the world.

FEBRUARY

1st   Brigid

Brigid founded the abbey at Kildare in Ireland in the sixth century. There are many stories about how she did various miracles (often involving the multiplication of food) and it is sometimes hard to tell which are true and which are not. Some stories even say that she was made a bishop. But she must have been a person close to God because of the way that people have honoured her for centuries.

3rd   Anskar

The King of Denmark in the ninth century became a Christian and wanted his country to be one that served God. He asked Anskar to work for him, evangelising his people. Anskar tried to stop the Viking slave trade and tried to give enough to the poor to make a difference to their lives rather than just to ease his conscience. He preached on a large scale, became an archbishop, and the people of Denmark made him their patron saint.

4th   Gilbert of Sempringham

Gilbert was someone who had vision for big things. He died in 1189 having built thirteen monasteries employing 1,300 people in all, but this had started from much less. Originally there had been just seven girls from his parish who lived in a house next to the church. But Gilbert added lay sisters and lay brothers and the Gilbertine order became established and remained that way until the Reformation. He was the only English person to found an order like that.

6th   The Martyrs of Japan

Christianity first came to Japan in 1549 with Francis Xavier, and fifty years later there were several thousand Christians there. The emperor felt threatened by them all and persecuted them, killing a group of 26 people. These included Paul Miki who was a Jesuit priest, two Jesuit lay

FEBRUARY

brothers, six Franciscans and seventeen lay people, including three young boys. The bodies had part of their left ears cut off to show everyone who they were.

10th   **Scholastica**

Scholastica loved God more than anything else. She got excited about the promises of heaven. We know this because she spent a whole night talking about it with her brother Benedict. She only saw him once a year, and on this occasion she prayed for there to be so much rain that he couldn't go home. God answered with a massive thunderstorm and it was just as well because she died only three days later (in c. 543). She was the first Benedictine nun.

14th   **Cyril and Methodius**

Cyril and Methodius were brothers who had particular gifts. They were good at talking to people in a relevant way, but they were also good at the academic side of things. They lived in the ninth century and invented what was later called the Cyrillic alphabet. They used it to translate liturgy and scripture into a language that people could understand.

14th   **Valentine**

Valentine was martyred on the 14th February in the third century. As far as we can tell, our present Valentine's Day customs have nothing to do with this person – they are more likely to be remains of a Roman festival which occurred mid-way through February. St Valentine seems to have been a bishop or maybe a priest, killed in a period of persecution.

15th   **Sigfrid**

Sigfrid was a monk at Glastonbury who was sent by King Ethelred to the King of Norway. Sigfrid worked in Sweden

FEBRUARY

too, and baptised the king. He did not choose to stay where it was easy, though, and worked in remote areas as well as the towns. God gave him a large capacity for forgiveness when his nephews were murdered; he pleaded for the lives of their killers and would not accept the money they gave as a fine even though he was very hard-up. He died in 1045.

15th Thomas Bray

Thomas Bray was rector at a church in Sheldon when he started to set up his library system in 1690. He established libraries organised by parish in England which was very important at a time when people could not afford many books. He was sent to Maryland for a while, but ended up working from England. His vision – for people to have access to quality Christian writing – eventually developed into the SPCK.

17th Janani Luwum

Janani Luwum was born to a poor Ugandan family in 1922. His parents were Christians, and he took his teacher training at a missionary college, but he was not converted himself until 1948. He was totally committed to human rights, knowing this was important to God. While he was archbishop he spoke out against the cruelties carried out by Idi Amin and his followers. Because of this he was shot dead – possibly by Amin himself.

23rd Polycarp

Polycarp was a strong and godly man who served God throughout his long life. He learnt from John the apostle, and his knowledge became vital to the second-century Church when heresies were everywhere. He loved Christ and was faithful to him even when faced by his death. This is shown by the way he treated the people who martyred him – he invited them for a meal and prayed for them before they finally killed him and burnt his body.

FEBRUARY

27th   **George Herbert**

George Herbert's poems express things about life and God which are deeper than the obvious and physical things which can be seen. He was able to go deep into truth and not be afraid of it. But he did not always plan on being a priest and a poet – he was an MP for a while and it seemed as if that was the way his career would go. When God called him, he ended up doing something completely different, but he knew that it was right. He died in 1633.

MARCH

1st   David, patron of Wales

David was a monk and a bishop who chose to live a life of austerity and works of mercy, in order to concentrate on the mysteries of God. The stories told about him show that he was a great inspirer from both his lifestyle and the way he preached – it is claimed that he founded ten monasteries, and was unanimously declared archbishop after a particularly stirring sermon. He died in c. 601.

2nd   Chad

Recognised by Bede as humble, devout, zealous and apostolic, Chad's good qualities shine. After a muddle over his first appointment as Bishop of Northumbria – he was consecrated by some rather dubious bishops – the archbishop had the good sense to give him another appointment, that of Bishop of the Mercians. Here Chad flourished, and under him so did his new bishopric, where he established a monastery and was so respected that he was revered as a saint immediately after his death in 672.

7th   Perpetua, Felicity and their companions

Perpetua, a young mother, and Felicity, her pregnant slave, along with three men, were arrested for the crime of being members of the Church. In 203 they were sentenced to death in the Games, to be killed by animals. As this terrible day drew near, though, they remained unafraid, experiencing visions as their faith grew, and eating an Agape meal together. As they went to face their death they were joyful, knowing that they were on their way to heaven.

8th   Edward King

An Oxford graduate, Edward went on to become Bishop of Lincoln. He came from a High Church background, but was prosecuted for illegal ritualistic practices. However, he was acquitted on appeal and kept his position – the

MARCH

trial made him more well loved than before. He was a Tory and active in politics, interested in youth and confirmations, and he published books of sermons and devotions to aid people's understanding of what happened in the Mass. He died in 1910.

8th   **Felix**

In 630 an exiled king returned to rule the East Angles, and Bishop Felix was called up to evangelise and care for the king's people. During the seventeen years that he held the post, he worked closely with both the king and Canterbury, giving the area stability and allowing God's work to happen unhindered. He founded a monastery at Soham, and showed great openness of mind when an Irish monk established another monastery nearby, as there is no record of conflict between the two.

8th   **Geoffrey Studdert Kennedy**

Geoffrey was ordained in 1908, and in the First World War was awarded the Military Cross. Later he became chaplain to the king, and messenger of the Industrial Christian Fellowship. He wrote poems and books showing that living as a Christian in the world was possible – that Christianity and modern life could continue hand in hand. Although he died in 1929, the things he wrote still inspire people today.

17th   **Patrick, patron of Ireland**

Patrick's experiences as a slave in a foreign land led him to rely deeply on God and to have a great aptitude to feel at home in any company. This was to stand him in good stead when in later life he returned to the land of his captivity as a missionary. There he developed good pastoral care and a real aptitude for stamping out paganism by adopting new meanings for old festivals so that all people could understand. He died in *c*. 460.

MARCH

18th   **Cyril**

Cyril was born in Jerusalem. When he became a priest his main job was to instruct new converts before and after their Baptism, and he became the author of a discipleship course, his most famous piece of writing. He became bishop in c. 349, and after further writing found himself accused of heresy, and was exiled and banished, although generally his writing is seen as merely exploring the faith.

19th   **Joseph of Nazareth**

Joseph was a man who clearly listened hard for God's solutions to insoluble human problems. With his wife pregnant before they were married, and his son causing upset in the highest circles, it was necessary for him to listen to God's solutions before taking action. He also had to be a man living closely with God to be able to cope with the responsibility of bringing up the Messiah. Through Joseph listening to him, God was able to bring all his plans to fruition.

20th   **Cuthbert**

Becoming a monk from a well-off Anglo-Saxon background in 651, Cuthbert soon became popular and rose to the position of prior. After the Synod of Whitby he changed to the Roman customs, and, as Prior of Lindisfarne, patiently drew the monks after him to get in step with the new customs in the Church. A period of time spent as a hermit gave him a reputation for great holiness, and led to his appointment as bishop. He became very active, preaching and visiting, and his holiness touched all those around him.

21st   **Thomas Cranmer**

Archbishop of Canterbury from 1533, Thomas used the opportunity of King Henry VIII's divorce to bring about a Protestant Church in England. He placed English translations of the Bible in parish churches so that all could understand its message, and was responsible for the Book of Common Prayer which put church services in a language

MARCH

all could comprehend and be part of. He was condemned for heresy under Queen Mary and was burnt.

24th   **Walter Hilton**

Born in c. 1340, Walter became an Augustinian monk at Thurgarton Priory where he explored the mystery of God. This led him to write a book, *The Scale of Perfection*, which was a methodical and easy-to-follow guide in two volumes on the improvement of one's soul and how to become a mystic.

24th   **Oscar Romero**

Oscar Romero was the Roman Catholic archbishop in San Salvador and was very aware of the troubles of the poor, campaigning ceaselessly on their behalf. Violence was rife, and Oscar constantly advocated God's peace and justice. However, what he was saying was disliked by many, and he was assassinated in 1980.

26th   **Harriet Monsell**

Following a very happy marriage, Harriet decided, after her husband's death, to live the rest of her life full-time for God. She moved to Clewer, Windsor, and came into contact with a group helping prostitutes. She formed a community to carry on supporting these women. Her enthusiasm and her warm heart encouraged people, and her original thinking solved problems. She was sometimes stern, but always ended a reproach with encouragement. She died in 1883.

31st   **John Donne**

Ordained in 1615, John is well known because of his poetry. His freedom of language used to explore his passion for God has enabled many readers to catch the vision and enter into the same passion. He also wrote theological essays and sermons which, rather than getting bogged down in theological disputes, are useful as they explore basic Christianity.

APRIL

1st   **Frederick Denison Maurice**

Frederick was a professor of literature at King's College, London, for a while and although he didn't have a degree, he was a writer and well respected. However, he was also determined to put across the truths about God without compromise, and some of the papers he had published about atonement and eternal life were not very popular. He had been professor of theology, but this title was taken away from him. He was also passionate about social justice and helped to found the Christian Socialist Movement. He died in 1872.

9th   **Dietrich Bonhoeffer**

Dietrich Bonhoeffer was very concerned that Christianity did not become simply a dry 'religion'. He wrote letters from prison about how Christianity should be relevant to the real world. He had been involved in a plot against Hitler and had determinedly campaigned against Nazism, which is why he had been imprisoned. He was hanged in 1945 for his views, and is remembered for his strength and courage.

10th   **William Law**

A Serious Call to a Devout and Holy Life is the book for which William is probably best remembered. He did not see his Christianity as something which could be taken half-heartedly or opted out of. The Wesleys were deeply influenced by this. William's life shows that he did take his faith seriously – when he was working at Cambridge University he would not swear allegiance to George I, as his obedience to God came first. This meant that he was forced to leave. He died in 1761.

10th   **William of Ockham**

William of Ockham was a Franciscan monk and a philosopher. He studied at Oxford and wrote a number of papers. His views were not always appreciated at the time – he felt that poverty was necessary for Christians, since Jesus

APRIL

had been poor, and he went against convention in saying Christians might stand against the Pope in certain circumstances. William was excommunicated, but held to his beliefs in spite of strong opposition. He died in 1347.

11th **George Augustus Selwyn**

Before 1841, New Zealand and Melanesia did not have a bishop at all. George was sent from England to do this job, and worked with the infant Church there, helping set up the constitution. He was organised and a good leader, and helped put the structures of the Church in place. He moved back to England after 26 years and became Bishop of Lichfield.

16th **Isabella Gilmore**

Isabella Gilmore was a reformer of the Anglican Deaconess Order. She saw the large numbers of committed women in church and wanted so much to see them used more. She had a distinct feeling of God calling her specifically to the work she did and knew that she wanted to serve him in worship and the way she worked with other people. She died in 1923.

19th **Alphege**

Alphege was made the Archbishop of Canterbury in 1005. He was a natural negotiator and had already worked for the king. But the peace he secured did not last for ever – in 1011 the Danes overran Southern England and took Alphege and others prisoner. They held them for seven months and demanded a ransom of three thousand pounds for Alphege, but he would not let anyone pay it. He was killed with ox bones, and is remembered as a martyr for justice.

21st **Anselm**

'Faith seeking understanding' was what encouraged Anselm to think through the things of God in a logical way. Anselm

APRIL

always took care to make sure he believed things because they were true. He wrote theological papers and was used by the Pope to defend the Church's doctrines with watertight arguments. He was made abbot at his monastery and later Archbishop of Canterbury. He always acted with integrity, and would never compromise what he thought was right. He died in 1109.

23rd **George, patron of England**

George is remembered as an example of all that is good about chivalry and noble behaviour. He was probably a soldier, and was martyred during the persecution of Christians in Palestine in the fourth century. But the qualities reflected in his legend are what people admire. He did not behave in a showy way for his own glory, but did what was necessary without expecting any reward.

24th **Mellitus**

After Augustine had brought Christianity to England, Gregory the Great felt that there needed to be further evangelism to reinforce the work that had been done. So he sent out a team of missionaries to England, with Mellitus to head them up. These people were the first to convert pagan temples and festivals to Christian usage, rather than destroying them completely. They realised it was important to value what was close to people's hearts, and to gently redirect their worship to the real God. Mellitus died in 624.

25th **Mark**

Mark was a friend of Paul, Peter (who calls him his 'son'), and Barnabas who was his cousin. He worked with them on their missionary journeys – sometimes there were arguments but they always kept their eyes on the goal of spreading the Gospel. Mark's mother was a Christian too,

APRIL

and she let the apostles meet in her house in Jerusalem. Tradition says that he became Bishop of Alexandria when he was older, and he wrote his Gospel helped by Peter's memories.

27th Christina Rossetti

In the bleak midwinter is a carol which has helped many people in worshipping God and giving all they have to him. Christina Rossetti wrote this, along with many other poems and hymns. She lived a life of service to God, and worked for a while at the London Penitentiary for Fallen Women, helping prostitutes to retrain for other jobs. She died in 1894.

28th Peter Chanel

Peter Chanel worked successfully as a priest and lecturer, but what he really wanted to do was to be a missionary overseas. In 1836 he was sent to some small islands near Fiji with a few helpers, and trusting in the power of God they healed the sick there. Although the people were known to be cannibals, they considered the missionaries as friends rather than food. Peter was killed when the chief objected to his son being baptised, but not long afterwards the whole island became Christian.

29th Catherine of Siena

Catherine felt called to a life of prayer even when she was young. It can't have been easy for her as she had over twenty brothers and sisters and her parents were quite unsupportive. She joined the Dominican order and tried to show God's love by caring for the sick. She also dictated letters about how people should be completely devoted to God. When she was older she spent her time helping to sort out the problems with Church politics which occurred in the fourteenth century.

APRIL

30th **Pandita Mary Ramabai**

An Indian social activist, Pandita believed that 'no caste, no sex, no work and no man' was to be depended on to achieve salvation, but that God gave it freely to anyone. She held to this idea of God's love and justice in the way she carried out her work. She spent a lot of time translating the Bible into languages that were accessible, carrying out her beliefs that the Gospel should not be just for people of a certain background or education. She died in 1922.

MAY

1st Philip

After becoming a disciple early on in Jesus' ministry, Philip was able to follow the growing development and realisation of who Jesus was, taking part in miracles and deep conversations. After Pentecost the facts become vague, but it is clear that after his life had been so touched by Christ he went to pass the blessing on to others. It is believed that he did this in Phrygia, and that his remains were buried with those of James.

1st James

James, often called 'the less', was another of Jesus' close friends and, together with Philip, experienced God in an amazingly close and personal way. An often-used title for him is the first Bishop of Jerusalem. If this is true, then it is clear that he did not believe his experiences with Jesus to be for him alone, but saw them as preparation to take the good news to the world.

2nd Athanasius

Athanasius, brought up in a Christian family and later becoming deacon and secretary to his bishop, gained a good picture of the views of the Church. This was consolidated further when he attended the first General Council, at which the Creed still used today was formulated. This knowledge stood him in good stead in 328 when he became bishop, as he wrote and taught extensively against the heresy that Jesus was not truly divine.

4th English saints and martyrs of the Reformation era

The period of time surrounding the establishment of the Church of England was a very bloody and tragic time for over-zealous members of both denominations. As different reigns changed the religious climate, yet more Christians suffered. Those who did were convinced that changing politics should not alter the way in which they worshipped God, and they counted their duty of worship as more important than their life. Amongst all the changes, true worship continued.

MAY

8th **Julian of Norwich**

Julian of Norwich is famous for her book *Revelations of Divine Love*. This came out of her experience of being very ill, seeing visions and being healed, with the first account being written soon after the experience, and the second written twenty or thirty years afterwards as she had spent time reflecting upon it. She became a recluse living in part of a church, but even though she was not living amongst people many still came to her for advice as she had such a degree of insight. She died in *c*. 1417.

14th **Matthias**

After the suicide of Judas another apostle was needed. Matthias, who had followed Jesus from his Baptism to his Ascension, and had seen Jesus after the Resurrection, was seen as a good candidate and was chosen for the post by drawing lots. After Pentecost there are traditions placing him preaching and teaching in places as far apart as Cappadocia and Ethiopia. Even though he came late into the apostolic mission, he did not let this deter him from taking a full part in fulfilling the role.

16th **Caroline Chisholm**

Caroline moved to Australia in 1838 where, moved by the problems of destitute immigrant girls in Sydney, she set up a home for them. She went back to England in 1846 to raise awareness and funds, but in 1854 moved back to Australia, this time inspecting the gold-fields and lecturing on the need for workers' safety. Her God-given compassion led to her pursuing a life very unusual for a woman at this time, and resulted in the improvement of conditions for immigrants.

19th **Dunstan**

After growing up in a noble family in the tenth century, a life in the court of the king was the natural progression for

MAY

Dunstan. However, after being expelled from the king's court, he became a monk and was ordained a priest. In Glastonbury he spent his time practising handicrafts before becoming abbot. During his three bishoprics he carried out a programme of monastic reform, which reformed the secular world as well. Throughout his life, involved in the politics of the day, he was not afraid to make his Christianity more than mere ritual.

20th Alcuin of York

Born in Yorkshire in *c.* 732, Alcuin moved to Tours where, as abbot, he founded a school in the abbey. It became a place where discussion could go deep and where knowledge could be passed on, with the arts encouraged as a way to better understand spiritual doctrine. Alcuin realised that the appreciation of beauty would lead to an appreciation of spiritual things, and in old age he gained a great reputation for holiness.

21st Helena

Coming to Christianity in 312 aged over sixty, Helena refused to allow her age to prevent her worship and threw herself into it with a zeal that made up for lost time. People who met her assumed that she had been a Christian all her life. With overflowing generosity, brought about by the love she felt from God, she helped churches, the poor and prisoners, and died on pilgrimage to the Holy Land, following Christ's footsteps to the last.

23rd Petroc

After uprooting himself from South Wales and moving to Cornwall, Petroc, who lived in the sixth century, established one monastery at Radstow, and thirty years later moved and founded another. After this time spent dealing with people and establishing community, Petroc became a hermit living on Bodmin Moor. Here he spent his time enjoying

MAY

the reflection of God's glory in creation. In his life of contrasts, he showed the ability to serve and enjoy God in any circumstance, both in company and alone.

24th **John and Charles Wesley**

These two brothers were brought up in a Christian home, and at Oxford University started a religious study group called the Holy Club where they went to Mass, discussed the Bible and served the wider community. Their methodical way of doing things earned them the nickname of Methodists. John went on to travel widely preaching, but the Church of England closed its doors to him as it could not cope with his enthusiasm. Charles translated the message of the Gospel into hymns, many of which are still sung and loved today. Charles died in 1788 and John in 1791.

25th **The Venerable Bede**

Bede, a student from the age of seven, really enjoyed learning and passing on what he knew. Although he probably never left Northumbria, he travelled extensively in his mind through both time and space as he wrote history books and commentaries on parts of the Bible. These grew out of the regularity of his monastic lifestyle with its times for reflection and for study. Although his life was not full of great 'events', God was able to use it to inspire a great output of useful writings. Bede died in 735.

25th **Aldhelm**

A monk from the Wessex royal family, Aldhelm became an abbot and then a bishop when the Wessex diocese divided in 705. Although from a wealthy family, he was able to utilise his learning to help people from many backgrounds. Writing in Latin, he covered the lives of saints and theology, and composing with a harp he created music to encourage people to come to church – in all this making religion accessible.

MAY

26th **Augustine**

Augustine, the reluctant missionary to the Anglo-Saxons, landed in Kent in 597. On his way he had nearly turned back but was urged to go on by Pope Gregory, the force behind the mission. After Augustine and his team of thirty monks had succeeded in converting the key figures in the kingdom, they erected a cathedral and a monastery. Through Augustine's co-operation with the vision, the truth had been brought to the Anglo-Saxons.

26th **John Calvin**

John Calvin was born in France in 1509 and went on to become a major figure in the Reformation and in establishing a Protestant Church. As a theological and ecclesiastical statesman and a reformer, he established a 'model' church in Geneva, and also wrote a treatise on Protestant belief. He was unafraid to think through ideas that had been held for a long time and to amend them where he felt necessary, and this enabled the Church to move forwards.

26th **Philip Neri**

After his conversion Philip left his job in business and went to Rome with no plans. He lived penniless in an attic for two years and studied for another three, and then began his life's work of introducing people to the faith he had found. At first informally with his friends and later as a priest, his charismatic personality made him approachable, and people opened up to him. Living in community with five other priests, and using an oratory for services, Philip brought many people to Christianity. He died in 1595.

28th **Lanfranc**

Lanfranc had known William the Conqueror before the conquest of England and there was mutual respect between them. After the conquest he became Archbishop of Canterbury and William's counsellor. He maintained excellent relations between the Church and the State, pressing for the Church's independence while living comfortably with the State. He also remained on friendly terms with the last main figure of the Celtic Church, Wulfstan. He died in 1089, having used his knowledge to be a peacekeeper.

30th   **Josephine Butler**

Josephine, born in 1828, grew up to be a key figure in the social reforms of the day. She gave her support to the beginnings of the movement to campaign for higher education for women, and in 1866, when she moved to Liverpool, she established homes for women at the bottom of society whom no one else would care for. She campaigned for the repeal and reform of laws, wrote pamphlets and books, and allowed God to awake her conscience.

30th   **Joan of Arc**

The daughter of a peasant farmer, and brought up during the Hundred Years War, Joan began at the age of fourteen to have visions about the future of France. Although it would have been easier for her to have ignored them, she knew that she must do what was right. After helping to bring about a number of French victories, the tide turned against her. However, even under persecution and the threat of death in 1431, she underwent her punishment bravely rather than go back on what she believed was God's will.

30th   **Apolo Kivebulaya**

Born the son of an escaped Muslim slave in c. 1864, Apolo became a Christian as a result of reading and writing lessons with a missionary. He became a missionary himself, teaching and setting up churches in Central Africa, with the language barrier treated as no obstacle. He became involved with the pygmy people in the forest, and was buried facing the forest to show how much he cared for them. He was very well loved because of the love he showed people.

JUNE

1st Justin

Justin's trial is carefully recorded in official Roman paperwork. He refused to deny his Christian beliefs and knew for certain that his death would not be the end. During his life he had been a philosopher, aiming to present the truths about Christ and the Church's practices in a way that was clear and logical. He felt that if anyone saw the truth presented in this way it would surely convince them. He died in c. 165.

3rd The Martyrs of Uganda

At the end of the nineteenth century, there was severe opposition to Christianity in Uganda and many people were martyred for their faith. A number of these were royal pageboys – the king had already killed one of them for teaching the others about Christianity, and the next day the others were called and ordered to identify themselves as Christians. They were all burnt to death. Other people were also killed for speaking out against the king's cruelty and corruption.

5th Boniface

Boniface was born in Devon in the seventh century. He worked for the King of Wessex as his link with the Archbishop of Canterbury. Later he turned down a job as an abbot because he felt that God wanted him somewhere else. The Pope then asked him to do missionary work, and it resulted in many people turning to Christianity. He was killed in 754 and was thought of as an important martyr by bishops of the time.

6th Ini Kopuria

Ini Kopuria was from the Solomon Islands, and in 1925 founded the Melanesian Brotherhood, a community for men within the Anglican communion. Members take vows of poverty, chastity and obedience, but for a certain length of time rather than for ever, and work as evangelists. It is the largest Anglican community for men.

8th Thomas Ken

Thomas Ken was a bishop in the seventeenth century. He was made chaplain to Charles II, but he was a strong person and he was not afraid to tell the king if he thought he was not doing the right thing. Charles wanted Thomas to move out of his house so that his mistress could have it, but he refused. He also stood up to James II when he became king – along with six other bishops he opposed the Declaration of Indulgence, which promoted Roman Catholicism.

9th Columba

Columba was the saint who went by sea over to Iona from Ireland and founded a number of monasteries. He was part of the Celtic tradition, in which all aspects of life are open to God and able to be holy. He was a determined person – some people think that he came to England in 'voluntary exile' or penance for mistakes he had made in Ireland. He is remembered as someone who was indispensable in bringing the English people to Christ. He died in 597.

9th Ephrem of Syria

Ephrem is remembered mainly because of all the things he wrote. He lived in the fourth century and made up hymns which were used in liturgy. In the first part of his life he was head of the Cathedral School in Mesopotamia, but when his home town was captured by the Persians he became a monk and lived in a cave. As well as writing, he was a practical person who organised help for famine victims.

11th Barnabas

Barnabas' name means 'son of encouragement', and he did seem to be able to encourage other people in their

JUNE

work. He introduced Paul to the twelve apostles (he was one of them) and became one of the first Christian workers. These people operated in the power of the Spirit, with only God, rather than tradition, backing them up.

14th Richard Baxter

The way that Richard Baxter looked after his parish was a model for many people after him. He saw pastoral care and counselling as just as important as preaching, and as a result his church grew and grew. The building actually had to be extended to fit everyone in. Although he had been ordained as an Anglican minister, he did not like the restrictions of the Church and allied himself with Puritans against this until the monarchy changed and everything became more relaxed. He died in 1691.

15th Evelyn Underhill

Evelyn Underhill was a poet and writer, born in 1875. Through the things she wrote she helped people understand that it was not only logical head-knowledge that mattered in their faith; experience was just as important. She led retreats from her late 40s and wrote in journals. Before she died she felt able to take on board some of the aspects of Christianity she had found difficult before, especially the institutional and sacramental side.

16th Richard, Bishop of Chichester

Many people remember how much God means to them when they pray Richard's prayer to know God more clearly and love him more dearly. Richard was a bishop and was very concerned to do his job in a way that honoured God and helped other people to do the same. He asked the people in his diocese to make sure they went to church on Sundays and holy days, and he would not let slackness or corruption creep into his clergy's behaviour. He died in 1253.

JUNE

16th Joseph Butler

The way that other philosophers argued in Joseph Butler's time made him sad. He knew that God was quite able to make himself known to us, but the Deists were saying that you had to trust nature rather than biblical promises, and Rationalists were explaining God away altogether. The things he wrote put the other side to these arguments, and he also gave practical advice on living selflessly – serving God just because he is God, and not for personal gain. He died in 1752.

17th Samuel and Henrietta Barnett

Just talking about social reform came far short of what Samuel and Henrietta felt called to do. Although they did write books – among them one called *Practicable Socialism* explaining how it all fitted in with Christianity – they carried out what they believed. They helped set up building programmes and cultural centres in the East End of London, where Samuel was a priest. Samuel died in 1913 and Henrietta in 1936.

18th Bernard Mizeki

It was not until he ran away to Cape Town that Bernard learnt about God at all. He studied at a mission school there, and when his teacher, Fräulein von Blomberg, told the class about how much God loved them, Bernard decided that he was going to serve God with all his heart. He went as a missionary to the Mashona people, and passed on his enthusiastic faith to them. When there was local trouble and violence, Bernard refused to budge, even though, in 1896, it resulted in his death.

19th Sundar Singh of India

Born to wealthy Sikh parents in India, Singh became a convert to Christianity. He was a mystic and saw the way

JUNE

that Christians should affect the world around them just as sandalwood affects its surroundings with its scent. He evangelised Tibet, and was very good at presenting Christianity in a way that touched chords with people who were from a Hindu background. He died in 1929.

22nd Alban

Even before he became one himself, Alban must have had some respect for people who were Christians – he helped to hide a priest who was trying to escape Roman persecution. This priest converted and baptised Alban, who swapped clothes with him so that he could get away. This meant that Alban suffered the punishment meant for the priest and was put to death in c. 250. Even though his faith was very new, he would not deny it to save his life.

23rd Etheldreda

Although Etheldreda was a king's daughter and her second marriage was to a king, she did not want to be wealthy. She left her husband because she wanted to stay a virgin – perhaps arranged marriages were not a good idea for a girl called to be a nun. She spent seven years living very simply, in prayer and penance. She died of the plague in c. 678, but seventeen years later her body was found to be whole and not decayed, which led to the development of her following.

24th John the Baptist

Undergoing considerable hardship to bring across his message of repentance and preparation for the coming of the Messiah, John lived in the desert wearing itchy, smelly clothes and eating locusts and honey. He was beheaded for standing up for what is right. This date celebrates his birth; his beheading is commemorated on 29 August.

JUNE

27th Cyril

Cyril was a theologian and bishop in the fifth century, a time when some of the Church's doctrines were still being worked through. He was important because he was able to defend the doctrine of the Trinity against people who thought that the parts of it were completely separate – three Gods rather than one.

28th Irenæus

Irenæus' main pieces of writing were not discovered until 1904, so most of the information about him has only been known for a relatively short time. He argued against gnosticism and for the authority of Scripture, and showed how the New and the Old Testaments fitted together. He lived in the second century and helped mediate when there were problems between Christian groups – he always was fair and listened to the whole story.

29th Peter and Paul

Paul was a fervent person; he wanted to do what was right more than anything else. He is remembered for his dramatic conversion, his missionary work and his letters. These are still considered an authority on practically everything – Paul was not afraid to lay down what was right, even if it was not what people wanted to hear.

Peter is one of the best-known of the apostles and was the leader of them. Many people are encouraged by the fact that, even though he denied Jesus when he said that he wouldn't, he was still able to go on to a powerful preaching ministry – stronger than he had been before. He was not as academic as Paul, but they were able to work together well in the cause of the Gospel.

JULY

1st Henry and John Venn

Henry Venn lived from 1725 to 1797 and his son John from 1759 to 1813. Both are remembered as key figures in the evangelical revival. Henry, much involved in it, wrote and preached sermons from this new way of thinking, and John, growing up in this atmosphere, became an evangelical vicar in Clapham. The circle of people he mixed with were nicknamed the 'Clapham sect' because their religious and social ideals were very distinctive, and from this grew his inspiration to found the Church Missionary Society.

3rd Thomas

Thomas, remembered for his doubts about the Resurrection of Jesus, encourages many who feel guilty for doubting, as his doubts led to the blossoming of strong faith. Traditionally it is believed that after Pentecost, Thomas went to India, telling people of what he had seen and introducing them to a living faith. It is believed that he was killed by a spear. His willingness to die for his faith proves that doubts can change into strength.

6th Thomas More and John Fisher

Thomas and John were two Roman Catholics who were executed in 1535 for refusing to take the oath of supremacy to Henry VIII as they believed that Henry was not the head of the Church. Although they both held high posts in the country – Thomas the Lord Chancellor and John the Bishop of Rochester they were willing to give up these, and even their lives, to do what they felt was right.

11th Benedict of Nursia

Benedict, the Abbot of Monte Cassino, realised that monastic life needed a rule to order it. Incorporating teaching on how monks should live from many different sources, Benedict formulated a rule that was famous and well used

JULY

for the simple fact that it worked. It encouraged monks to have a balanced existence of prayer, reading and manual labour, and came to be used all over Europe, with later rules inspired by it, its influence spreading far beyond Benedict's death in c. 550.

14th   **John Keble**

John was one of the founders of the Oxford movement which attempted to bring the Church of England back to its High-Church roots. In 1827 he wrote a book of poems for Sundays and feast days, as he felt that beauty aided worship. He was also the author of tracts arguing against state control of the Church and encouraging people to read the Early Church fathers so they would not lose their theological insights.

15th   **Swithun**

Swithun, a Wessex man, was chosen by King Egbert to be his chaplain and to educate his son. When the son became king, it was Swithun he chose to be the Bishop of Winchester – obviously Swithun's holiness had impressed the boy. His time as bishop was made difficult from the first attacks by the Vikings, but he still succeeded in consolidating the importance of Wessex. Famous for his great charity and for building churches, he died in 862.

15th   **Bonaventure**

Bonaventure became a Franciscan in 1243. After several teaching appointments, he was elected Minister-General of the Franciscan order, and brought the order back from chaos by defending Franciscan ideals but giving them a structure. He was also a theologian, rather more interested in the mystery of God than just dogma. It appears from contemporary accounts of him that he was not only a successful theologian and leader of people but also an easily accessible man.

JULY

16th Osmund

In early life, as king's chaplain and chancellor, and later as Bishop of Salisbury, Osmund excelled in administration. He loved books, copying and binding them by hand, and learning new things. Osmund also took part in the preparation of the Domesday Book and in other pieces of royal administration before his death in 1099. A skilled man, he used the talents that God had given him for their best effect and revelled in their use.

18th Elizabeth Ferard

Elizabeth visited the Lutheran Deaconess Institution in Germany in 1858 which so inspired her that on arriving back in England she set up an Anglican equivalent. It began in 1861, with women living together under a rule whilst serving God in the larger community, teaching, nursing and working in parishes, with the authority of being ordained deaconesses. Elizabeth's vision and determination resulted in an order which helped the community and enabled women to fulfil their vocations.

19th Gregory of Nyssa

Gregory was first a professor of rhetoric at Athens, but later became disillusioned and left. He became a monk and later an unsuccessful Bishop of Nyssa. However, he was more successful in writing intellectual theological works, and it is these for which he is chiefly remembered. He forms an important link in the transmission of the work of Origen, an early Christian thinker, to later times, and his ideas are still read today. He died in 394.

19th Macrina

Macrina, Gregory's older sister, devoted herself to living a Christian life. When her brothers and sisters were younger she helped to look after them, and after they were grown she lived a monastic life. It is partly from the influence of

JULY

Macrina that three of her brothers, including Gregory and Basil, became the men they did, and so her influence on the Early Church was massive. She died in c. 379 completely confident and free of fear.

20th   **Margaret of Antioch**

Possibly only a fictional character, Margaret is still a well-known saint. The legend says that she was the daughter of a pagan priest who became a Christian and was thrown out of her home. Somebody tried to marry her but she refused, even when tempted and tortured in various ways. She travelled around preaching and converting large numbers of people before being beheaded. Her determination to resist temptation meant that she could be completely used by God.

20th   **Bartolomé de las Casas**

Bartolomé went to Grenada as a soldier, was rewarded with land, and evangelised the Indians living on it. He was disgusted by the ill-treatment that the Indians suffered and decided to do something about it. In 1515 he returned to Spain to plead their cause, but was really rather ineffectual. However he did not give up, calling for the abolition of slavery, and writing against the sin of domination, oppression and injustice.

22nd   **Mary Magdalene**

There is a dispute over who Mary Magdalene is. She might be either the woman who anointed Christ's feet or the sister of Martha and Lazarus. Because of this she is remembered both for the forgiveness given to repentant sinners and also as an advocate for the contemplative life. It is certain, though, that whoever she was, she was one of the first people to see Jesus after he had risen from the dead.

23rd   **Bridget of Sweden**

At the age of fourteen, Bridget was married and went on to have eight children. She was summoned to court to be

JULY

the queen's lady-in-waiting, and began to have supernatural revelations, but the king and queen did not reform, and the other members of the court just gossiped. After her husband died, she founded a monastery where all excess wealth was given to the poor. Leaving it in 1349 to go to Rome, she never returned but instead spent her time travelling and serving people.

25th   James

James was one of Jesus' most intimate friends, witnessing Jesus' transfiguration and the raising of Jairus' daughter – events which must have deepened his faith. The fact that he was killed with a sword by King Herod Agrippa shows that the time he had spent with Jesus had so convinced him of the truth of what Jesus had said that he was willing to die for it. As the first apostle to be put to death, his courage must have encouraged the others.

26th   Anne and Joachim

Anne and Joachim, the parents of Mary, are not known from historical details but rather from the life of Mary their daughter. We know that Mary, only young when pregnant with Jesus, must have been brought up to be self-reliant and to worship God with all her being. Anne and Joachim must have been open-minded to be able to support their daughter in her pregnancy, and the way they brought Mary up must have partly influenced her ability to say 'yes' to God.

27th   Brooke Foss Westcott

The Bishop of Durham and a scholar, Brooke Foss is famous for several academic works, including a translation of the Greek text of the New Testament – a major source for the English Revised Version of the Bible, commentaries and a history of the New Testament canon. He was also very interested in social issues, calling a conference for European

JULY

Christians in 1889 as a response to the arms race in Europe, and mediating in the Durham coal strike of 1892.

29th Mary, Martha and Lazarus

Mary, Martha and Lazarus were two sisters and their brother who were very close to Jesus. The Gospels say that Jesus visited them, and, while they discussed things, revealed in various ways who he was and what he had come to do. When Lazarus died, Jesus cried, but went on to raise him to life again, showing his power over death. Legend has it that they evangelised Provence, although this is unlikely. What is likely is that their close friendship with Jesus immensely affected their lives.

30th William Wilberforce

William was remembered more for being good company than as a scholar while at Cambridge, but, regardless of amazing intellect or not, he went on to become a very influential political figure. He became a Christian in 1784-5, and this led him to a deep love of his fellow people. He believed that God loved all equally, and that this should influence our laws. From 1787, he entered into the struggle against the slave trade and slave ownership, and, largely from his campaigning, the laws were changed.

31st Ignatius of Loyola

Ignatius started off life as a soldier, but, injured in battle, he read the life of Christ while getting better, and became a Christian. After a period of study, he and six disciples took vows of poverty, chastity and serving the Pope. They carried out works of charity, teaching and being missionaries, and were given papal approval in 1540. They became known as the Jesuits, and by the time Ignatius died, in 1556, they were working across Europe and into the rest of the world.

AUGUST

4th **Jean-Baptiste Vianney**

Jean-Baptiste Vianney was a priest in France in the nineteenth century. He is the patron saint of parish priests. He spent much of his time – twelve or thirteen hours a day – listening to people's confessions, as people would travel from miles away to see him. He was available to God to be useful, and started to see people healed when he prayed for them.

5th **Oswald**

Oswald became a Christian at Iona when he was in exile. He was able to return home to Northumbria some years later when the king who had defeated him died. Oswald wanted Northumbria to be a Christian country, so he asked Aidan to work for him. Aidan was well loved and led many people to faith in Christ. Oswald was martyred in 642 after only eight years of rule, and his body was offered, in pieces, to the god Woden. It was not long, however, before people found his remains and made a Christian shrine to them.

7th **John Mason Neale**

John Mason Neale was an Anglican priest. He wrote his own hymns but he also translated a lot of hymns which were in Latin or old words which people could not understand. Many medieval and ancient hymns were translated by him – he did not want people to miss out just because the language they used was different. He made sure that the words were still beautiful, poetic and full of meaning. He died in 1866.

8th **Dominic**

Dominic started his life as a priest in a way which prepared him for what he was called to do later. He spent seven years quietly in prayer and penance before he became prior. People wanted him to become a bishop, but Dominic knew that God wanted something different. He founded an order of friars who were not obliged to do manual work and so were available for teaching.

AUGUST

9th **Mary Sumner**

The Mothers' Union was founded in 1876 after a speech by Mary Sumner at the Portsmouth Church Congress. She had seen the need for an organisation which supported families in their difficult jobs, and wanted to have a group of women in every place who were able to pray together and 'seek by their own example to lead their families in purity and holiness of life'.

10th **Laurence**

Laurence died as a martyr in 258, traditionally believed to have been roasted on a gridiron, but more probably killed with a sword as that was what was used for execution at the time. Together with Stephen, he is the patron of deacons. One of his jobs was almsgiving, and he is often pictured with a purse of money in his hand.

11th **Clare of Assisi**

Clare decided to become a nun when she was eighteen and heard Francis preaching. At first she joined the Benedictines, but after a few years she was able to move into a building near the church Francis had rebuilt. She became the abbess, and her mother and two sisters joined her there. Clare, who died in 1253, outlived Francis by 27 years, and although she sometimes suffered with illness quite badly, she remained serving her community and praising God.

11th **John Henry Newman**

In the nineteenth century the Oxford Movement was started to encourage true 'catholicism' in the Church of England. John Newman was very involved with this. Later he actually became a Roman Catholic. He wanted to be true to the Church and make sure that it was what it was supposed to be. He wrote poems and hymns too – *Lead, kindly light* is one of many.

AUGUST

13th **Jeremy Taylor**

In the 1650s there were a lot of political disturbances, and many people in the Church of England were not able to hear a priest preach very often. Jeremy Taylor wrote a couple of books to help them – *The Rule and Exercises of Holy Living* and *The Rule and Exercises of Holy Dying*. Even a century later, John Wesley was using these books. Taylor was made Bishop of Down and Connor in 1660 and served on the Irish Privy Council.

13th **Florence Nightingale**

Although she was brought up to be an educated young lady, Florence did not want to use her advantages to get away from the world's horrors and sufferings. She knew God had called her to something, and after a few years she realised what it was. She trained as a nurse and was asked to take a group of other nurses to look after soldiers wounded in the Crimean War. The conditions were terrible, but Florence is remembered for the way she knuckled down and cleaned the place up, always working for the comfort of her patients. She died in 1910.

13th **Octavia Hill**

The National Trust was founded by Octavia in 1895 – a result of her vision for people to have open space and pleasant surroundings available to them. She also worked in slum areas, improving housing. She led a number of projects and trained other women to work in the area of housing provision. At the time she was working, the cities' populations were growing rapidly and she knew how crowded the environment could be.

14th **Maximilian Kolbe**

When Kolbe was in Auschwitz, one of the other inmates he knew was condemned to death. Kolbe was a Franciscan friar, without a family, and he volunteered his own life in

AUGUST

this man's place. This showed just how much he was living out his faith in Christ. He had been put in the prison camp because he had helped Jewish refugees and stood up against the Nazi regime. Honouring Mary was an important part of his faith – she was someone, like him, who had given her whole life to God.

15th   Mary

Mary is remembered as someone who was completely available to God – whatever that might involve. She did not make excuses or ask for time to think about it when the angel said she would have a baby. She must have been worried that she might not have been good enough, but she knew God well enough to understand that he would be the one to give her everything she needed to do the job properly.

20th   Bernard

When he was 22, Bernard joined the Cistercian order along with 31 of his friends. They joined the abbey at Citeaux, even though it was in a financial mess and near to closure. This saved the monastery and Bernard became the abbot a few years later. He helped the Cistercian order to expand – at his death in 1153 there were 400 houses in Europe. He led the failed second crusade, but he is remembered for his contributions to monastic life more than for that.

20th   William and Catherine Booth

William and Catherine set up the Salvation Army together in 1865. They started the Christian Mission in Whitechapel, which met with considerable opposition at first, but as the ideals of the Salvation Army became known, the organisation became loved and respected. They wanted to get rid of squalor and poverty, and show people how faith in God could change their whole outlook on life.

AUGUST

24th   Bartholomew

Bartholomew was one of the twelve apostles. It is thought that he worked in India and Armenia – a copy of Matthew's Gospel was left there which was thought to have been left by him. He was martyred for his faith – suffering a horrible death by being flayed alive.

27th   Monica

Monica was the mother of Augustine of Hippo. She had a difficult household with a violent and unfaithful husband, and a mother-in-law who lived with them and added to the conflict. Augustine refused to follow Christianity too. But Monica hung on to God through it all and prayed patiently for them. Her husband became a Christian a year before his death, and Augustine travelled to Rome and was baptised there. Monica's devotion and commitment paid off. She died in 387.

28th   Augustine of Hippo

Augustine was an intelligent person. He studied philosophy for many years, but he felt that the things he learnt contradicted Christianity. He turned away, although he had been brought up a Christian. But his mother, Monica, did not give up praying for him, even when he always won the arguments. Eventually, he realised that Christianity was true, and accepted it wholeheartedly. He used his philosophical training to explain Christian truths instead. He died in 430.

30th   John Bunyan

Earlier in his life, John Bunyan had felt that his sins were too terrible and he was outside God's grace, but gradually God showed him that it was not like that – he was forgiven. He wrote *Pilgrim's Progress* from the perspective he had gained from the difficult times he'd had spiritually, and from his twelve years in prison for carrying out a service

AUGUST

that was not legal in the Church of England. It has spoken to people for many centuries now. He died in 1688.

31st **Aidan**

Aidan was asked by King Oswald to come and evangelise Northumbria in 635 after the previous bishop had run into difficulties. He moved from Iona to Lindisfarne and began preaching, often with Oswald himself as interpreter. He encouraged lay people to fast and meditate on the Scriptures, and made sure that he did not accumulate things he did not need.

SEPTEMBER

1st Giles

Giles, born in the early seventh century, became a hermit in Provence. King Wamba gave him some land on which to build a monastery. This became a popular place to visit, as a place to stop on the way to Compostella and the Holy Land, as well as a destination of the pilgrimage itself. This reputation must have come about because of the holiness of Giles which impressed and inspired the visitors.

2nd The Martyrs of Papua New Guinea

In 1942, the Japanese invaded Papua New Guinea. There were many missionaries living and working there, and the invasion had been imminent for some time. Most missionaries had been evacuated, but of those who stayed over 200 died, many of them executed by the Japanese. Their bravery in staying stemmed from the fact that they knew that they were where God wanted them, and that this was where they should stay despite the consequences.

3rd Gregory the Great

Gregory became a monk in 574, but then was called out of the monastery by the pope to become a deacon and then an ambassador. After six years he returned to the monastery as abbot, but then, during an outbreak of the plague, was called to become pope himself. He had always wished to lead a mission to the Anglo-Saxons, but now he willingly delegated to others. He produced many writings, cared for other churches and sorted out problems, going under the title of 'servant of the servants of God'.

4th Birinus

Sent to England to carry on the mission to the English, Birinus taught the King of Wessex about Christianity, and became Bishop of Dorchester. He was an active bishop, baptising many people over the fifteen years he was at

SEPTEMBER

Dorchester, and building churches around the area. Even with little or no support from Canterbury (as there was probably no contact between them), Birinus still did much in his life before he died in 650.

6th Allen Gardiner

In his 30s, Allen left the navy to join the mission field. He wasn't sure where he wanted to go and tried Zululand and New Guinea before settling on South America when he founded what was later known as the South American Mission Society. The society was very short of funds with its first three trips a complete shambles. The fourth reached where it was meant to, but everyone on it died of exposure, with Allen writing suggestions for improvements before his death in 1851.

9th Charles Fuge Lowder

Ordained priest in 1844, Charles felt strongly that an Anglo-Catholic way of worshipping, with beauty and lots of ceremony, really helped people to get close to God. Undeterred by riots against the ceremonial nature of his services, he took part in the first regular mission work in East London. This work grew and the people of East London were converted in their thousands. To have such an effect, Charles must have loved his parishioners, and he was always known as Father Lowder – a mark of affection as well as respect.

13th John Chrysostom

Brought up in Antioch with a good education, John went first into a monastery and then became a priest back in Antioch. Here he cared for the city's poor, and in his Bible commentaries tried to apply the Bible to real life problems. In 398 John became Archbishop of Constantinople, reforming the morals in Church life and outside it. His plain speaking angered the empress and he was exiled, dying en route.

SEPTEMBER

15th Cyprian

Cyprian was a brilliant orator and teacher, and after his conversion in c. 245 he gave up all remnants of his pagan religion and concentrated his skills solely for God. He became a priest, and when forced to leave his people because of persecution, led them by letter. When he came back, some had lapsed, and he dealt with this sensibly, giving them time to come back. Under the next persecution in 258, Cyprian was executed.

16th Ninian

Ninian founded a monastic college at Whithorn, with many ideas apparently coming from Martin of Tours whom, legend has it, he visited on his way back from Rome. He was a very influential figure in the conversion of the southern Picts, and the monastery he built was obviously a place steeped in prayer. He believed that the point of studying was to enable people to see God reflected in his creation. He died in c. 432.

16th Edward Bouverie Pusey

Edward, born in 1800, became an influential figure in the Oxford movement. As well as writing tracts and preaching sermons, he was interested in practical caring, helping the sick in a cholera epidemic in 1866. In 1845, he helped to found the first Anglican sisterhood which played a major part in bringing back the monastic life into the Church of England. His life shows that a passion for theology can easily lead to an interest in practical caring.

17th Hildegard

Hildegard was educated by a recluse and became a nun at the age of fifteen. She started to have visions and explanations for them from God, and became abbess of

SEPTEMBER

Diessenberg. Here she wrote down her visions as well as other works, including commentaries and natural history. Her down-to-earth holiness brought many people to her convent, which became so large that it had to be moved, and many people came to her for spiritual direction. She died in 1179.

19th   Theodore of Tarsus

A Greek by birth, Theodore was asked to go to England to become the Bishop of Canterbury in 666. England was in a troubled state after the Synod of Whitby and a recent outbreak of the plague, but Theodore still went. Even though he was 65 when given the post, as archbishop he visited most of the country, made sure that vacant positions were filled, set up a school and held the first synod of the Anglo-Saxon Church.

20th   John Coleridge Patteson and his companions

John, born in 1827, was educated at Eton and Oxford. His father was a judge, but in 1855 John became a missionary. He spent sixteen years in the New Hebrides, Banks, Solomon and Loyalty Islands, and in 1861 was consecrated Bishop of Melanesia. He spent ten years working amongst the people in the islands, but on one visit to an island was killed by its inhabitants along with his companions.

21st   Matthew

Matthew, originally a tax-collector working for the Romans, became one of Jesus' apostles and worked for God's kingdom instead. He probably wrote Matthew's Gospel, which concentrates heavily on the human links in the story of Jesus. This must have been a reflection of how he dealt with people, believing that all were special and seeing how God's plan was revealed through time through the people who loved and listened to him.

SEPTEMBER

25th   **Lancelot Andrewes**

Lancelot, who lived from 1555 to 1626, became a theologian in a very unstable period in the Church of England. There were many different theological streams influencing the Church, and although Lancelot came across Puritan influences in Cambridge, he decided to toe the middle line between Calvinistic dogmatism and Puritanical reformation. As well as being a theologian, Lancelot was a court preacher. Although acknowledging different streams of theology, Lancelot was secure enough to draw a happy medium.

25th   **Sergei of Radonezh**

A refugee as a boy, Sergei became a monk, restoring his first monastery and re-establishing community life. In 1334, he was chosen as superior, but discontent over his strictness led to him leaving. He went on to found forty monasteries in his lifetime, all along the same lines of a common life. The visitors to his monasteries found a great impression of moral strength, which emboldened them to go and live moral Christian lives outside cloister walls.

26th   **Wilson Carlile**

Wilson inherited his family silk business, but after it was ruined in a slump in the markets, he was ordained. He wanted the Church to develop more contact with the working classes, as he believed that it was those at the bottom of society that the Church was there for, and in 1882 he established the Church Army. In its training colleges, lay people were trained to carry out social work, and Wilson's work stimulated the Church to be more aware of social issues.

27th   **Vincent de Paul**

Ordained at the age of nineteen, Vincent combined his ministry with the rich with that of service for the poor. In

SEPTEMBER

1625 he founded the Lazarists, a group of priests from all backgrounds who would serve people no matter what their status. In 1633 a body of women was set up who would serve the ill and poor – the Sisters of Charity. The way in which he loved all people with a God-given love must have allowed many to experience the love God had for them.

29th **Michael and all angels**

Michael and the other angels, although not sharing our humanity, can lead us on to worship God with more enthusiasm, love and awe, and can remind us of the part we play in the struggle against evil. Michael gets a special mention for being an archangel, but as we go around our daily lives we can remember and join in the worship that is constantly going on amongst all the angels in heaven.

30th **Jerome**

After being a hermit for five years, and later working in Rome, Jerome moved to Bethlehem where he started a community of monks and began translating the Bible. He believed that the translation should go back to the roots as far as possible, that it should be well explained, and that monastic life should be based on the study of this. Although his argumentative personality made him many enemies, his translation enabled many to understand the Bible.

OCTOBER

1st **Remigius**

When he was only 22, Remigius was made Bishop of Reims. He was friends with King Clovis (and his wife Clotilda who was already a Christian), and helped him on his way to becoming a Christian. Clovis' conversion came about after his son was cured of an illness and the army won a battle which it really looked as if it should lose – both after prayer. Remigius baptised thousands of soldiers and founded many churches, and when he prayed for people he often saw them healed. He died in 523.

1st **Anthony Ashley Cooper**

Many social reforms were put in place in the nineteenth century, and Ashley was involved in a number of these. Because of his place in the House of Commons he was able to get things done. He put through bills to stop people having to work ridiculous hours at the mills and children under ten from working in the mines. He also was president of the Ragged Schools Union which saw 300,000 children educated for free.

4th **Francis of Assisi**

Francis is one of the best-loved saints. He is remembered as someone who was gentle, honest, and close to the heart of a loving God. Earlier in his life he had been a soldier and quite wealthy, but God called him to give all that up and live in poverty. As people saw his life, they joined his work and the Franciscan order grew from there to the worldwide organisation it is now. He died in 1226.

6th **William Tyndale**

William Tyndale was convinced that people needed access to the Bible to learn about God. He felt that this should be what determined what the Church did, rather than half-remembered legends or customs. He set to work in

OCTOBER

the 1520s translating the New Testament into vernacular English, but he had to keep moving around to avoid arrest. He was put to death in the end, but even by the time he died fifty thousand copies of his translation had been distributed.

9th **Denys**

Denys is the patron saint of France. He was sent, along with six other bishops, to Gaul by the Pope. He was made bishop of Paris, and helped convert the people to Christianity. When the Roman Emperor Valerian started persecuting Christians, Denys and his companions were some of the people to be martyred. He was killed in 258.

9th **Robert Grosseteste**

In the thirteenth century, when Robert was working as a bishop, many of his colleagues were being given placements because they were working for the government. Robert saw this as wrong – he knew that these were separate things and felt that the integrity of the Church should not be compromised in this way. Members of both sides disagreed with him on occasions, but he stuck to what he believed was right. He also made many translations into Latin from the Greek and Aramaic.

10th **Paulinus**

Paulinus came to England in 601, sent by Gregory the Great. He was chaplain to Ethelburga who had married the King of Northumbria. The king was not a Christian at the time, but a few years later was converted and baptised by Paulinus. This all happened at a time when many people who had been pagans were wanting to get baptised. Paulinus himself had baptised the pagan high-priest.

OCTOBER

10th   **Thomas Traherne**

The poems of Thomas Traherne tried to express the feelings of excitement and wonder that many people feel when they are children. He wrote about the things of God in a way that helped people experience them. He wrote prose too – meditations to help people get closer to God. Many of his manuscripts were lost for over two centuries until they were found, by chance, in a London bookstall in 1896.

11th   **Ethelburga**

Ethelburga was the Abbess of Barking in the seventh century. She may have actually owned the abbey as well, since she was from a wealthy – and perhaps royal – family. A traditional story says that she learnt how to live in holy orders from the person who was to be her successor, but although it was all new to her, she seemed to fit in and a number of miracles were attributed to her.

11th   **James the Deacon**

When Paulinus was evangelising Northumbria between 625 and 633, James was there beside him, helping in his work. When Paulinus retired and King Edwin – who had supported them – was killed, James stuck it out and carried on working there. He baptised people and taught them about Christianity, even though the rulers of the time made it difficult.

12th   **Wilfrid of Ripon**

Wilfrid lived in the seventh century. He felt it was important that the Celtic Church did not develop separately from the Roman Church, and made sure that the Roman practices were followed. He was imprisoned for a while because of this, but was able to work in Sussex later. He helped many people become Christians and founded a monastery at Selsey.

OCTOBER

12th   **Elizabeth Fry**

Elizabeth was a Quaker minister who helped reform the prison system. She travelled around Britain, making reports on the conditions in different prisons. She made suggestions for improvement, many of which were taken up. These included female supervision for female prisoners, access to religious instruction and other education and the right to employment.

12th   **Edith Cavell**

During the First World War, Edith worked as a nurse, looking after soldiers who were injured. She helped many of them escape to the Netherlands, which was a neutral country, and hid them at the Red Cross hospital where she worked. She was executed for doing this, and many people protested because she had only been helping them, not actually spying.

13th   **Edward the Confessor**

It was not always an easy life for Edward who was botn in c. 1003. When he was young, he had been sent to Normandy to live with people who were jealous of him, and his mother actually tried to stop him when he became king. He tended to have mood swings and snap at people, but as his name implies, he always tried to get right again with God afterwards. He did not allow it to be a long time before doing this, and tried not to let the barrier of sin build up.

15th   **Teresa of Avila**

When twenty-year-old Teresa joined the Carmelites, it was normal for nuns to be supported by some sort of endowment from a wealthy person. Teresa saw nothing wrong with this at first and got on with her life in the convent. At the beginning she was ill for a while and spent a lot of time praying, but when she recovered she stopped. It was

OCTOBER

not until fifteen years later that God showed her what she should really be doing. Then she began to reform the Carmelite order, encouraging prayer and contemplation, and living purely on public alms. She died in 1582.

16th Nicholas Ridley and Hugh Latimer

'We shall this day light such a candle, by God's grace, in England as I trust shall never be put out.' These were the words of Latimer to Ridley as they were about to be burnt at the stake for heresy in 1555. They had been leaders of the Reformation, refusing to agree to the need for veneration of the saints, the existence of purgatory or the doctrine of transubstantiation. They were strong in their beliefs until death, and would not let go of what they believed was true.

17th Ignatius of Antioch

Ignatius lived in the first century and was a very important person in the establishment of the Early Church. He fought against heretics who said that Jesus had suffered and died 'only in appearance', and Judaisers who did not accept the New Testament. He saw that the Church needed structure – a hierarchy – and to be functional and organised, and this was carried out. He was arrested by the Roman authorities and thrown to wild animals in the arena, but he never denied his faith.

18th Luke

The Gospel of Luke and the Book of Acts were most probably written by him. He travelled with Paul, working with him and teaching people about Jesus. He speaks excitedly of the exploding Church in Acts, obviously enthusiastic for anything God's service would throw at him. He was probably a doctor, and writes with the precision that would be expected from someone with that job.

OCTOBER

19th **Henry Martyn**

Henry Martyn worked as a chaplain for the East India Company in the early nineteenth century. He travelled with them to India, Persia and all that area of the world, and must have honed his local language skills as he went along – he translated the New Testament into Hindustani, Hindi and Persian, the Psalms into Persian, and the prayerbook into Hindustani. He died when he was only 31, but he had achieved much by then.

25th **Crispin and Crispinian**

These two brothers were martyred in about 287 by the Emperor Maximian. They were from a rich family, but travelled around preaching the Gospel and supporting themselves by making shoes. Many people became Christians because of meeting them. Because of their profession, they were made the patron saints of shoemakers.

26th **Alfred the Great**

Alfred was a king but he was also a scholar. He loved Latin and learnt it so that he could translate books into English for his people. He translated Pope Gregory's *Pastoral Care* – a manual for priests – and may have translated the first fifty Psalms. He encouraged all young freemen to learn to read English, with the primary aim that they would be able to understand God's will and grow in wisdom. He died in 899.

26th **Cedd**

In the seventh century there were still a large number of people in Britain who had not heard about Christianity. Cedd worked in Bradwell and Tilbury in Essex, spreading the Gospel, and was well appreciated. He was made a bishop like his brother Chad, and both were at the Synod of Whitby in 663-4. Cedd was the translator there. He was given land for a monastery at Lastingham and fasted for forty days before he consecrated it.

OCTOBER

28th   **Simon and Jude**

Simon and Jude were apostles, so they knew Jesus well, and they are said to have evangelised Persia when the Church was young. According to tradition, Simon was martyred by being cut in half with a saw. They were both Zealots – members of the Jewish nationalistic party – at the time when they were working with Jesus.

29th   **James Hannington**

James Hannington was the first Bishop of Eastern Equatorial Africa. He had been a priest in England, but when he heard about two missionaries who had been killed he realised the urgency of this work. He went out to Uganda, but had to come back because he was ill. Eventually, in 1885, he got to Lake Victoria, where the missionaries had been killed. The King of Uganda heard that he was there and had him killed too within a few days. He was a brave person who was not put off by dangerous things.

31st   **Martin Luther**

Luther's 95 theses, which he pinned to the door of his Church in 1517, were the centre of controversy and discussion in his time and led to a shake-up in the Church as a whole. Luther was unhappy with the shortcomings of the Roman Catholic Church of the time. God had shown him how it was grace alone that was needed for salvation – not any series of rituals which humans could do. He was also well aware of the need for clear biblical teaching, and did this in his own church as far as he could.

NOVEMBER

3rd Richard Hooker

At an early age, Richard showed intellectual promise and was sent to Oxford. He was ordained in 1581 and got married. He was given the mastership of the Temple, but there was a degree of controversy over the post, so he moved. A theologian, he ended up writing eight books on the *Laws of Ecclesiastical Policy* which were central in influencing the tone and direction of the theology of the Anglican Church.

3rd Martin of Porres

Martin left his apprenticeship to a barber-surgeon to join the Dominicans. He became a lay helper, and the brothers were so impressed by his holy life that he was invited to become a lay brother. He spent his nights praying, and this time spent alone in God's company led him to a very loving lifestyle in the daytime. He cared for all people who came to him, regardless of what race or colour they were, as he realised that all were loved by God.

6th Leonard

A Frankish noble living in the sixth century and used to power, influence and the good life, Leonard became a Christian. His godfather Clovis offered him a bishopric but he turned this down, with all the status it conferred, to live as a monk and then alone as a hermit in a solitary cell in a forest. There Clovis' wife had a child safely under the care and prayers of Leonard, whose sacrifices for God had led to deep faith.

6th William Temple

William, ordained in 1909 even after doubts over doctrine, went on to become both the Archbishop of York and of Canterbury following in the footsteps of his father who had been Archbishop of Canterbury too. He was very

NOVEMBER

involved in social issues, especially education and unemployment, and became a Labour party member. He was also concerned for Church unity, believing that nothing should impede the Gospel message. He wrote books explaining the faith, and died in 1944.

7th **Willibrord of York**

Born in Yorkshire, Willibrord went on to be a key figure in the conversion of Holland and Luxembourg. He showed great bravery in killing sacred cows to feed his hungry people, and in destroying idols even though it was a threat to his life to do so. He energetically brought the Gospel to people, based not just on mere enthusiasm but on enthusiasm which was tempered and refined by prayer and a knowledge of the Bible. He died in 739.

9th **Margery Kempe**

Born in 1364 and becoming the wife of a burgess and mother of fourteen children, Margery underwent a period of insanity which led to her conversion. She went on numerous pilgrimages, and dictated a book which was a kind of spiritual autobiography – *The Book of Margery Kempe*. This shows that she counted spiritual matters as much part of life and of just as much importance as physical ones. She died in c. 1440.

10th **Leo the Great**

Leo, elected bishop of Rome in 440, was behind many of the accepted doctrines of the Church. He wrote a statement on the Incarnation in 451, and another explaining the humanity and divinity of Christ and how they combined in Jesus. He was also a major political figure, protecting Rome from invasion and sacking, although in this he was less successful. Leo was good at thinking things through clearly, and being able to get other people to understand them, without losing any of the meanings.

NOVEMBER

11th **Martin**

Martin faced troubles on account of his faith very soon after becoming a Christian. He had been in the army, but when he tried to leave, feeling fighting was inconsistent with the life Jesus had preached, he was imprisoned. He was later released, and in Amiens gave half of his cloak to a beggar as he realised not only other people's needs but also his own. As a monk-bishop, he worked in the hitherto unreached countryside, and died c. 397.

13th **Charles Simeon**

Born in 1759, Charles became an evangelical priest, and a fellow and perpetual curate of King's College, Cambridge. He was a really gifted preacher, and known over large areas. It was really Charles who spearheaded the evangelical revival in the Church of England, opening up the Church to new and revitalising influences. Charles also helped to form the Church Missionary Society in 1793. He died in 1836.

14th **Samuel Seabury**

Born in Connecticut and educated at Yale College and Edinburgh University, Samuel lived in the United States of America during the War of Independence. Although he held loyalist sympathies, after the peace he became a loyal citizen of the United States. He became the first Anglican bishop in North America in 1783, and influenced and shaped the constitution and liturgy of the Protestant Episcopal Church. He held strong views, but was able to be humble with them.

16th **Margaret**

Margaret, a refugee after the Norman conquest, married Malcolm III of Scotland while taking refuge in his court. She spent lots of time praying and reading, and meditating over her sewing, and these things made her a very loving

NOVEMBER

and generous person. Malcolm, who originally was rather coarse, saw through his love for his wife the motivation behind everything she did, and saw in her the love of Jesus, and changed. Margaret died in 1093.

16th   Edmund Rich of Abingdon

After studying in Oxford and in Paris, Edmund became Archbishop of Canterbury in 1233. He hated the politics and administration that went with the role, but instead of doing it all badly himself, this led him to pick people to do these things who were really talented in those areas, which meant that everything got done well. He stopped the king from interfering and managing the Church badly, and also got the Church moving politically to avert civil war.

17th   Hugh

As Bishop of Lincoln, Hugh was a friend both to the oppressed and to kings. When there was anyone in trouble, he was on their side. When the kings demanded things that were wrong, Hugh refused – although in the nicest way. He founded schools, extended the cathedral, held synods, and was a very hands-on bishop. He believed that lay people could live just as holy lives as monks and nuns, and that they were just as important.

18th   Elizabeth of Hungary

Elizabeth, born in 1207, was a very generous person, and was happily married with three children. However, in 1227 her husband Louis died of the plague. She underwent intense mourning, missing him dreadfully, and left her life of being generous from the confines of the court to become a tertiary Franciscan, helping people not lavishly but simply. Her spiritual director was very harsh and nasty, but she kept on loving people cheerfully.

NOVEMBER

19th Hilda

Hilda lived for 66 years, half in secular life and half in monastic life. After her involvement in several different abbeys, Hilda founded Whitby, an abbey for both monks and nuns. It became famous for the learning that went on in it, and for the wisdom of Hilda herself. She hosted the Synod of Whitby, employing her skills as peacekeeper between the two sides. She died in 680.

19th Mechtild

From when she was twelve years old, Mechtild started having visions and revelations from God. She became a nun at Magdeburg, and started writing them all down in books. She was not always well, and was always being threatened with her work being burnt. She went back to her family for a while because of this, and later joined a convent where there were other women who had visions so she was not on her own. She died in 1280.

20th Edmund

Edmund was born in 841, brought up as a Christian, and became King of East Anglia. When the Vikings invaded, bringing their pagan religion with them, he led an army against them. He was defeated and captured, but refused to deny his faith as he knew that it was the truth. Edmund was probably offered as a sacrifice to the Viking gods, but in reality had given his life for the one, true God.

20th Priscilla Lydia Sellon

In 1849, Priscilla founded the Society of Sisters of Mercy of the Holy Trinity at Devonport, Plymouth. This was only the second Anglican sisterhood to be founded. Some people strongly criticised her work, and other people supported her, but she is now remembered as someone who reformed the Church when it needed it.

NOVEMBER

22nd — Cecilia

Cecilia was one of the people to be martyred in the early Christian Church. She had vowed to God that she would stay a virgin, and explained this to her arranged husband. He said that he would respect this as long as he could see the angel who had given her the message. She told him to be baptised, and then he did see the angel. His brother became a Christian too. She gave everything she had to the poor, but this led to the order for her death. She was put in a fire, but the flames did not touch her, and she was beheaded instead.

23rd — Clement

According to the stories about Clement, he was such an effective Bishop of Rome, evangelising and leading the Churches, that he was exiled to the Crimea. His evangelistic skills were not confined to Rome, as in exile it is claimed that his preaching won so many converts that they had to build 75 churches to put them all in. He was thrown into the sea with an anchor around his neck and drowned in c. 100, but his life had shown many people the life of Jesus.

25th — Catherine of Alexandria

Being a well-educated girl from a noble family, Catherine knew the wife of the emperor and had influence in the royal family. She converted the emperor's wife, but Maxentius himself was not so open, to put it mildly. He led the persecutions against Christians in the fourth century, and sent scholars to argue with Catherine about her faith. She was not daunted by them, but Maximian had her put to death – first on a spiked wheel which broke, and then beheaded.

25th — Isaac Watts

When I survey the wondrous cross and *O God, our help in ages past* are two of Isaac Watts' most famous hymns. He

NOVEMBER

was a congregational minister for quite a while, but had to give it up because he was ill. He was still able to write, however, and wrote a number of hymns. Later on he wrote a book about reason and the search for truth, which was popular for a long time even after his death in 1748.

30th **Andrew**

Andrew, originally a fisherman, had been a follower of John the Baptist, but when Jesus came on the scene became one of his disciples. Although we do not know where he went after Pentecost, there are several places that claim him as their apostle. Because of this, it is safe to say that he did go on to this ministry, and that God really did use him to fish men instead of fishes.

DECEMBER

1st **Charles de Foucauld**

Charles lived as a hermit in the Sahara desert. The things he said are remembered because they were very wise. He considered no work beneath him because he wanted to be like Jesus, not considering himself better than anyone else. One of the things he wanted to see people (including himself) doing was to 'cry the Gospel with their whole lives'. He wrote about prayer too, saying that the important thing was not the form of the prayer, but the love with which it is said. He died in 1916.

3rd **Francis Xavier**

There are areas of Japan and India which are still Christian because of the work of Francis Xavier and his companions. He always kept certain principles in mind when doing his mission work – to adapt to the customs and languages of the people he was working with, and to have clergy from the local population who had been properly educated. His vision was to evangelise China, but he died of a fever in 1552 before he could get there.

4th **John of Damascus**

John of Damascus lived in the eighth century. He was a theologian, and wrote a number of books about what God was like. He also wrote defending the practice of venerating icons. He became a monk and spent his life writing and preaching. Because of this he was known as 'the Golden Orator'.

4th **Nicholas Ferrar**

A friend of George Herbert, Nicholas Ferrar was someone else who pressed on with God, not being content to remain passively where he was. In his earlier life he mixed with royalty and accompanied the Queen of Bohemia to Holland. But he gave that all up and became a deacon, founding a community with his relatives, and subsisting by making books. He died in 1637.

DECEMBER

6th   Nicholas

Saint Nicholas, better known as Santa Claus, was a fourth-century bishop in what is now Turkey. He was put in prison for a while during the persecution of Christians, but was released in time to go to the second Nicean Council. He was a generous person – one story says how he gave marriage dowries in gold to three girls who would otherwise have been forced to make a living through prostitution.

7th   Ambrose

Ambrose, a seventh-century bishop, could see the way that the Roman empire was heading. He knew, however, that the Church did not have to collapse too – he saw it instead rising 'like a growing moon' above it all. He was firm and fair in his duties as a bishop – he would not let people behave in an immoral way, but he was also compassionate. He was often able to secure reprieves for people condemned to death.

13th   Lucy

Lucy was one of the many people who were martyred during the persecutions under Diocletian in the early fourth century. Traditionally, the story goes that she refused to marry, and was sentenced to death – first by fire, which would not hurt her, and then by being pierced in the neck with a sword. Some of the earliest British churches were dedicated to her.

13th   Samuel Johnson

Samuel Johnson is best remembered for his English Dictionary, which he put together without the experience of a degree (he was not actually a doctor although many people called him by that title). He was often short of money and wrote one of his moral books in a week to offset the

DECEMBER

funeral expenses when his wife died. He wrote carefully and he was a real and human person – his biography by his friend James Boswell shows this side of his character. He died in 1784.

14th   John of the Cross

Through his poems, John of the Cross was able to help people experience the reality of the Resurrection and meet with God. He lived in Spain in the sixteenth century and worked with Teresa of Avila in restoring the Carmelite Order. On two occasions he was put in prison for this, but he carried on with his poetry there.

17th   Eglantine Jebb

When Eglantine was 24 she started travelling, trying to improve the conditions of the places she went to and the places she returned home to. Her work gradually developed into the Save the Children Fund; she raised millions of pounds which helped to provide food for children who did not have any. In 1924 the League of Nations passed the 'children's charter' which supported her principles.

26th   Stephen

Stephen was the first Christian martyr, stoned to death in 36. He had been working as a deacon for the Early Church community – he was one of the seven people chosen to sort out the community care for the elderly widows who were missing out on the distribution of food. He was especially gifted as an evangelist, and his discussions with many important Jews – and their conversion – was what got him into trouble with the Sanhedrin.

27th   John the Apostle

Revelation, the three letters and the Gospel of John are all traditionally thought to have been written by John the

DECEMBER

Apostle. He was one of the disciples closest to Jesus, and may have been describing himself as the 'disciple whom Jesus loved' in his Gospel. He died at an old age in Ephesus.

29th Thomas Becket

Thomas Becket became adviser to King Henry II because the archbishop – his friend Theobold – recommended him. At first he and the king worked well together, but they fell out over matters of policy. Henry wanted to take authority for the State which Thomas felt belonged to the Church. Thomas was killed by some of Henry's knights who had taken some of his angry words too literally. He was cut down and killed in Canterbury Cathedral in 1170.

31st John Wyclif

In 1376 John Wyclif wrote a book which made quite a few people feel rather uneasy. In it he said that all authority – in Church or State – is given by the grace of God, and that rulers who took advantage of that in a cruel or selfish way did not deserve to lead. He thought that both authorities should be accountable to one another. He did not like the way that some church practices had developed into no more than a ritual, and he emphasised the importance of religion from the heart.

ALPHABETICAL LIST

Name	Page		Name	Page		Name	Page
Aelred of Hexham	5		Ferard, Elizabeth	38		Mary (sister of Martha)	41
Agnes	8		Ferrar, Nicholas	68		Mary Magdalene	39
Aidan	47		Fisher, John	36		Matthew	51
Alban	34		Fox, George	6		Matthias	25
Alcuin of York	26		Francis de Sales	8		Maurice, Frederick Denison	19
Aldhelm	27		Francis of Assisi	54		Mechtild	65
Alfred the Great	59		Francis Xavier	68		Mellitus	21
Alphege	20		Fry, Elizabeth	57		Methodius	12
Ambrose	69		Gardiner, Allen	49		Michael	53
Andrew	67		George	21		Mizeki, Bernard	33
Andrewes, Lancelot	52		Gilbert of Sempringham	11		Monica	46
Anne	40		Giles	48		Monsell, Harriet	18
Anselm	20		Gilmore, Isabella	20		More, Thomas	36
Anskar	11		Gore, Charles	7		Mungo (Kentigern)	6
Antony of Egypt	7		Gregory of Nazianzus	4		Neale, John Mason	42
Aquinas, Thomas	9		Gregory of Nyssa	38		Neri, Philip	28
Athanasius	24		Gregory the Great	48		Newman, John Henry	43
Augustine	28		Grosseteste, Robert	55		Nicholas	69
Augustine of Hippo	46		Hannington, James	60		Nightingale, Florence	44
Azariah, Vedanayagam Samuel	4		Helena	26		Ninian	50
Barnabas	31		Herbert, George	14		Osmund	38
Barnett, Henrietta	33		Hilary	6		Oswald	42
Barnett, Samuel	33		Hilda	65		Patrick	16
Bartholomew	46		Hildegard	50		Patteson, John Coleridge	51
Basil the Great	4		Hill, Octavia	44		Paul	35
Baxter, Richard	32		Hilton, Walter	18		Paulinus	55
Becket, Thomas	71		Hooker, Richard	61		Perpetua	15
Benedict of Nursia	36		Hugh	64		Peter	35
Bernard	45		Ignatius of Antioch	58		Petroc	26
Birinus	48		Ignatius of Loyola	41		Philip	24
Biscop, Benedict	6		Irenæus	35		Polycarp	13
Bonaventure	37		James	24		Pusey, Edward Bouverie	50
Bonhoeffer, Dietrich	19		James	40		Ramabai, Pandita Mary	23
Boniface	30		James the Deacon	56		Remigius	54
Booth, Catherine	45		Jebb, Eglantine	70		Rich, Edmund	64
Booth, William	45		Jerome	53		Richard, Bishop of Chichester	32
Bosco, John	10		Joachim	40		Ridley, Nicholas	58
Bray, Thomas	13		Joan of Arc	29		Rolle, Richard	8
Bridget of Sweden	39		John of Damascus	68		Romero, Oscar	18
Brigid	11		John of the Cross	70		Rossetti, Christina	22
Bunyan, John	46		John the Apostle	70		Scholastica	12
Butler, Joseph	33		John the Baptist	34		Seabury, Samuel	63
Butler, Josephine	29		Johnson, Samuel	69		Sellon, Priscilla Lydia	65
Calvin, John	28		Joseph of Nazareth	17		Selwyn, George Augustus	20
Carlile, Wilson	52		Jude	60		Seraphim of Sarov	4
Catherine of Alexandria	66		Julian of Norwich	25		Sergei of Radonezh	52
Catherine of Siena	22		Justin	30		Sigfrid	12
Cavell, Edith	57		Keble, John	37		Simeon, Charles	63
Cecilia	66		Kempe, Margery	62		Simon	60
Cedd	59		Ken, Thomas	31		Slessor, Mary	5
Chad	15		Kennedy, Geoffrey Studdert	16		Stephen	70
Chanel, Peter	22		Kentigern (Mungo)	6		Sumner, Mary	43
Charles	10		King, Edward	15		Sundar Singh of India	33
Chisholm, Caroline	25		Kivebulaya, Apolo	29		Swithun	37
Chrysostom, John	49		Kolbe, Maximilian	44		Taylor, Jeremy	44
Clare of Assisi	43		Kopuria, Ini	30		Temple, William	61
Clement	66		Lanfranc	28		Teresa of Avila	57
Columba	31		Latimer, Hugh	58		Theodore of Tarsus	51
Cooper, Anthony Ashley	54		Laud, William	5		Thomas	36
Cranmer, Thomas	17		Laurence	43		Timothy	9
Crispin	59		Law, William	19		Titus	9
Crispinian	59		Lazarus	41		Traherne, Thomas	56
Cuthbert	17		Leo the Great	62		Tyndale, William	54
Cyprian	50		Leonard	61		Underhill, Evelyn	32
Cyril (Bishop of Jerusalem)	17		Lowder, Charles Fuge	49		Valentine	12
Cyril (brother of Methodius)	12		Lucy	69		Venerable Bede	27
Cyril (Bishop of Alexandria)	35		Luke	58		Venn, Henry	36
David	15		Luther, Martin	60		Venn, John	36
de Foucauld, Charles	68		Luwum, Janani	13		Vianney, Jean-Baptiste	42
de las Casas, Bartolomé	39		Macrina	38		Vincent de Paul	52
Denys	55		Margaret	63		Vincent of Saragossa	8
Dominic	42		Margaret of Antioch	39		Watts, Isaac	66
Donne, John	18		Mark	21		Wesley, Charles	27
Dunstan	25		Martha	41		Wesley, John	27
Edmund	65		Martin	63		Westcott, Brooke Foss	40
Edward the Confessor	57		Martin of Porres	61		Wilberforce, William	41
Elizabeth of Hungary	64		Martyn, Henry	59		Wilfrid of Ripon	56
Ephrem of Syria	31		Martyrs of Japan	11		William of Ockham	19
Ethelburga	56		Martyrs of Papua New Guinea	48		Willibrord of York	62
Etheldreda	34		Martyrs of Uganda	30		Wulfstan	7
Felicity	15		Martyrs, Reformation era	24		Wyclif, John	71
Felix	16		Mary	45			